© 2024 Jordan Daniels and Mia Daly
All rights reserved.

No part of this book may be reproduced or transmitted in any form or by any means, electronic or mechanical, including photocopying, recording, or any information storage and retrieval system, without permission in writing from the publisher.

Published by Piano Pal LLC

Printed in China
ISBN 979-8-218-48013-4

This product complies with all applicable safety standards, including the Consumer Product Safety Improvement Act (CPSIA), ASTM standards, and Federal Communications Commission (FCC) regulations. For more information about compliance and safety, please visit https://www.pianopalllc.com/the-magical-musical-forest-adventure

For piano tutorial videos and audio files, please visit:
https://www.pianopalllc.com/the-magical-musical-forest-adventure

Note to Parents and Guardians:

It's recommended that your child reads this section together with you. Learning about music can be a fun and rewarding experience, and your support will help them understand and enjoy these new concepts!

Piano Fingering Basics

Piano fingering is about which fingers to use to play the piano. Each finger has a number.

- Thumb: 1
- Pointer: 2
- Middle finger: 3
- Ring finger: 4
- Pinky: 5

Please try to practice the pieces with the recommended piano fingerings, placed above the notes. Note: For this beginner piano book, you will be using only your right hand.

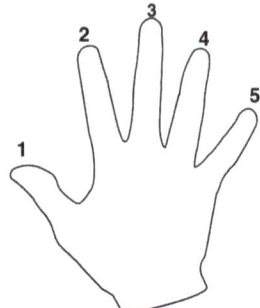

Learning Notes with Colors

When you play the piano, each key makes a different sound called a note. To help you learn, we'll use colors for each note. Look at the colored stickers on your piano keys (if you're using an external piano, we recommend adding colored stickers like in this image):

- C = Red
- C#/Db = Pink
- D = Orange
- D#/Eb = Yellow Orange
- E - Yellow
- F = Green
- F#/Gb = Light Green
- G = Blue
- G#/Ab = Light Blue
- A = Magenta
- Bb = Light Purple
- B = Purple

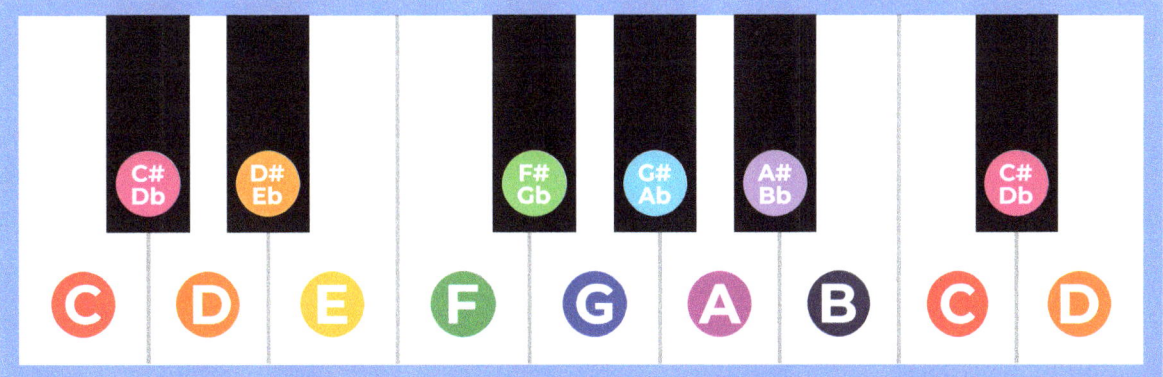

What Do Sharps (#), Flats (b), and Naturals Mean?

- **Sharp (#):** A sharp means you play the note a half step higher. For example, C# (pink) is a half step higher than C (red).

- **Flat (b):** A flat means you play the note a half step lower. For example, Bb (light purple) is a half step lower than B (purple).

- **Natural (♮):** is used in music to cancel a sharp (#) or flat (b) and return a note to its original pitch. If a note was sharp (#), the natural brings it back down. If a note was flat (b), the natural brings it back up.

Understanding the Treble Clef

The treble clef is a symbol you'll see at the beginning of music written for higher notes. It looks like a fancy, curly "G".

The Treble Clef Staff

Music is written on a set of five lines called a staff. The treble clef tells us which notes to play on these lines and spaces.

See how the color of the notes match the colors of the stickers on the keyboards.

Understanding Time Signatures

Time signatures tell us how music is organized. They look like two numbers, one on top of the other, at the beginning of a piece of music.

What Do the Numbers Mean?

- **Top number:** Tells you how many beats are in each measure (a measure is a small section of music).•

- **Bottom number:** Tells you what kind of note gets one beat.

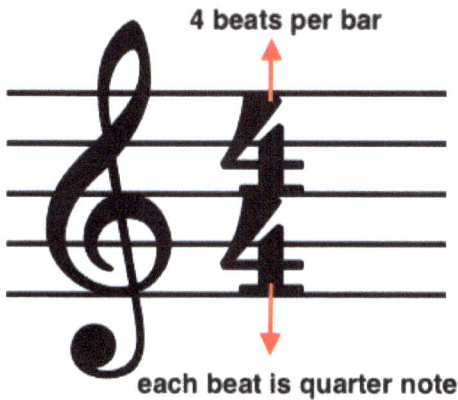

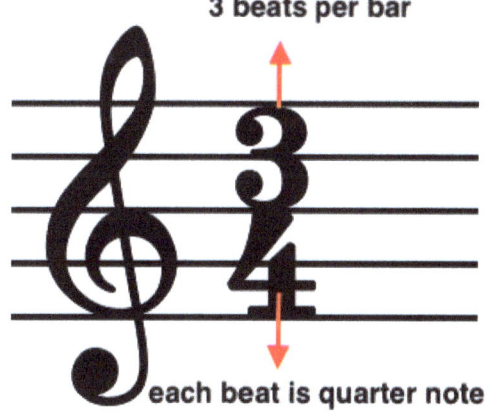

Understanding Key Signatures

A key signature is a set of sharp (#) or flat (b) symbols placed at the beginning of a piece of music, right after the clef. It tells you which notes to play as sharps or flats throughout the music.

 One flat indicates each B (purple) should be played as a B flat (light purple).

 Two flats indicates each B (purple) should be played as a B flat (light purple) and each E (yellow) should be played as a E flat (yellow orange),

 One sharp indicates each F (Green) should be played a F sharp (light green).

Understanding Beats and Note Values

In music, understanding beats and note values is crucial for grasping rhythm and timing. Here's a basic overview of common note values:

Whole Note:

- Value: 4 beats
- Description: A whole note lasts for four beats and fills an entire measure in 4/4 time .It's represented as an open circle without a stem. When you see a whole note, hold it for the full duration of the measure.

Dotted Half Note:

- Value: 3 beats
- Description: A dotted half note lasts for the duration of a half note (2 beats) plus an additional half of that value (1 beat), totaling 3 beats. It is represented as an open circle with a stem and a dot placed to the right of the note.

Half Note:

- Value: 2 beats
- Description: A half note lasts for two beats. It's represented as an open circle with a stem. In a 4/4 time signature, two half notes fit into one measure. Hold each half note for two beats.

Dotted Quarter Note:

- Value: 1.5 beats
- Description: A dotted quarter note lasts for the duration of a quarter note (1 beat) plus an additional half of that value (0.5 beats), making a total of 1.5 beats. It is represented as a filled-in circle with a stem and a dot placed to the right of the note.

Quarter Note:

- Value: 1 beat
- Description: A quarter note lasts for one beat. It's represented as a filled-in circle with a stem. In 4/4 time, four quarter notes fill a measure. Hold each quarter note for one beat.

Quarter Rest:

- Duration: A quarter rest lasts for one beat.

- How to Play: When you see a quarter rest in your music, you stay silent for one beat. Imagine taking a short pause before continuing to play.

Half Rest:

- Duration: A half rest lasts for two beats.

- How to Play: When you see a half rest in your music, you stay silent for two beats. It's like taking a longer pause before moving on to the next note.

Tie

- Definition: A tie is a curved line that connects two notes of the same pitch. It indicates that you should play the first note and hold it for the combined duration of both notes.

- How to Play: When you see a tie, you play the first note and do not play the second note separately. Instead, you hold the first note for the total length of both notes connected by the tie. For example, if a quarter note (1 beat) is tied to another quarter note (1 beat), you hold the note for 2 beats.

GET STARTED AND HAVE FUN!

Now that you know the basics, you're ready to start playing and exploring music. Look for these symbols and colors as you play, and remember to have fun! Keep practicing, and enjoy your journey with the piano. You're doing amazing!

One bright and sunny afternoon, Max and Mia were playing in their backyard when they heard the most beautiful piano music coming from the forest behind their home. Intrigued and enchanted, they asked their parents if they could explore and then decided to embark on an adventure through the magical musical forest. They knew it was going to be an adventure of a lifetime.

MARY HAD A LITTLE LAMB

Wandering through the fields, they met a sweet girl named Mary who was singing about her little lamb. Mary sang "Mary Had a Little Lamb" and showed the children how to play the song on a mini piano she gave them. The lamb, with a twinkle in its eye, guided them to the next part of their journey.

MARY HAD A LITTLE LAMB

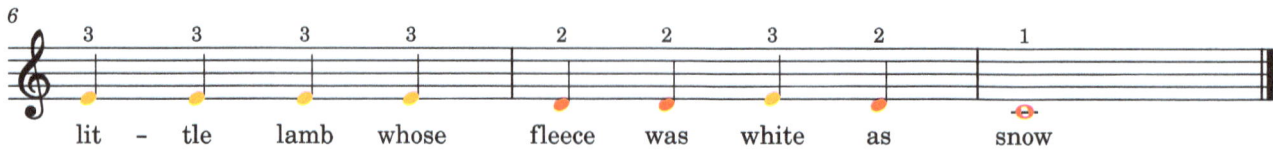

SHE'LL BE COMING ROUND THE MOUNTAIN

Following the lamb's directions, the children found themselves on a winding path around a grand mountain. As they walked, they heard the song "She'll Be Coming Round the Mountain" echoing in the air. They played along on their piano, the lively tune keeping their spirits high as they traveled.

SHE'LL BE COMING ROUND THE MOUNTAIN

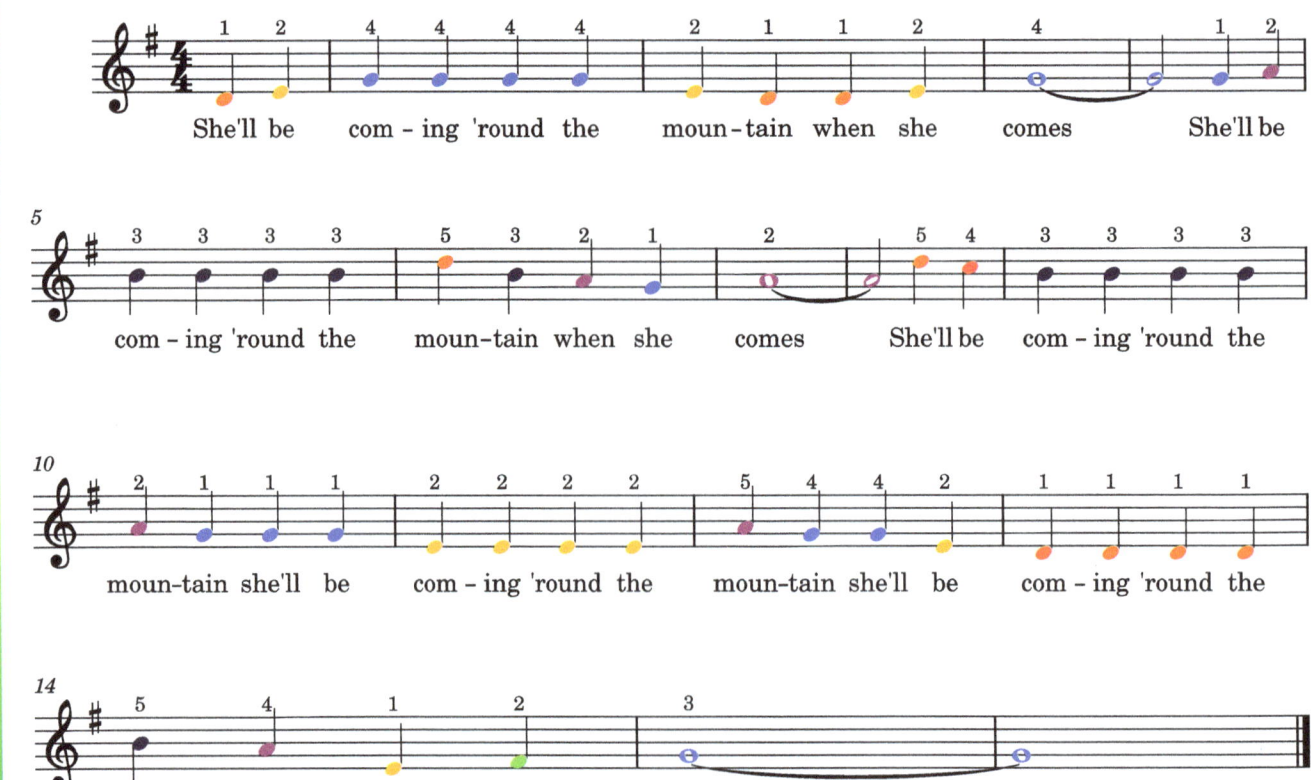

OLD MCDONALD HAD A FARM

The trail led them to a whimsical farm, where the animals were not only talking but also singing. A jolly cow greeted them and started singing "Old McDonald Had a Farm." The children watched in amazement as each animal joined in, and they quickly learned the notes to play along on their mini piano.

OLD McDONALD HAD A FARM

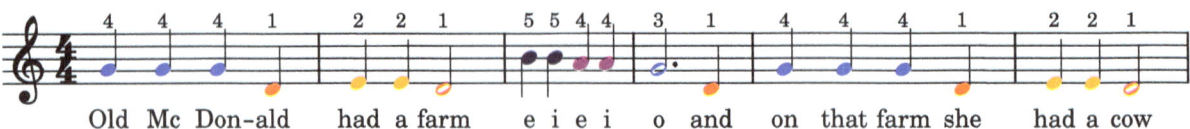
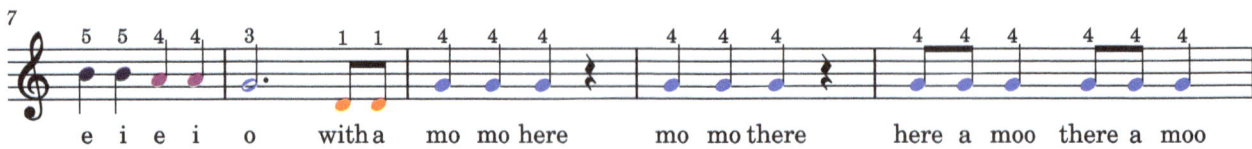

FIVE LITTLE MONKEYS JUMPING ON THE BED

Exploring the farm further, they came across a lively scene of five little monkeys jumping on a bed of hay. The monkeys were laughing and singing "Five Little Monkeys Jumping on the Bed." The children joined the fun, playing the melody on their mini pianos, and learned the playful tune as they watched the monkeys' antics.

5 LITTLE MONKEYS

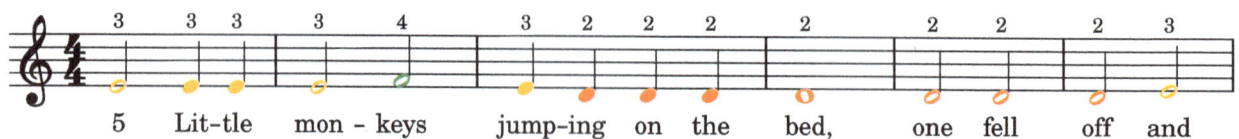
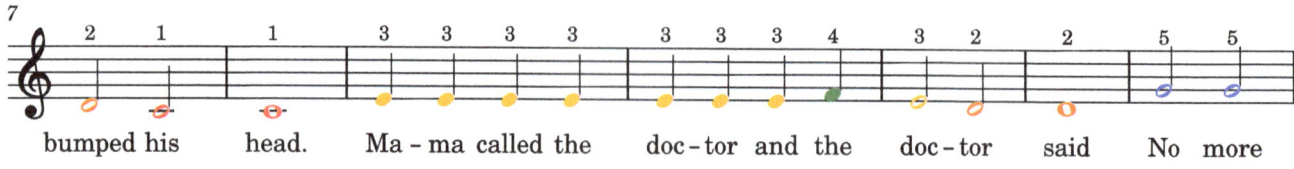
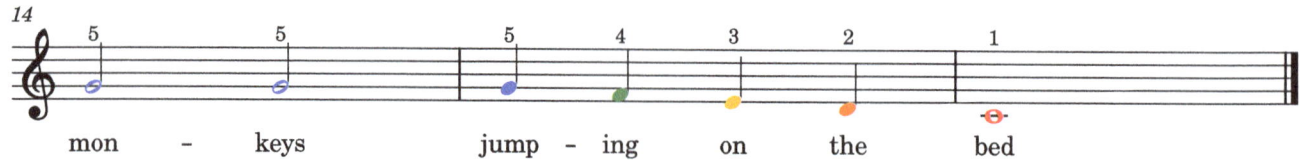

THE ANTS GO MARCHING

As they stepped into the forest, they noticed a formation of ants marching in perfect harmony. The ants, with tiny instruments in their hands, began to sing "The Ants Go Marching One by One." The children couldn't help but march along, learning the rhythm of the song as they followed the ants deeper into the woods.

THE ANTS GO MARCHING

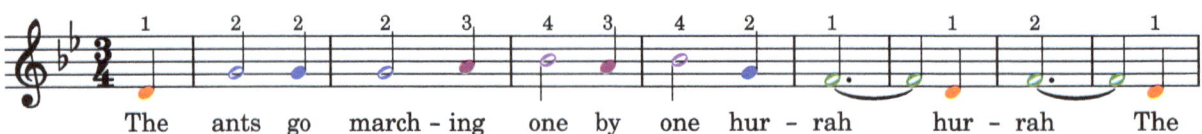
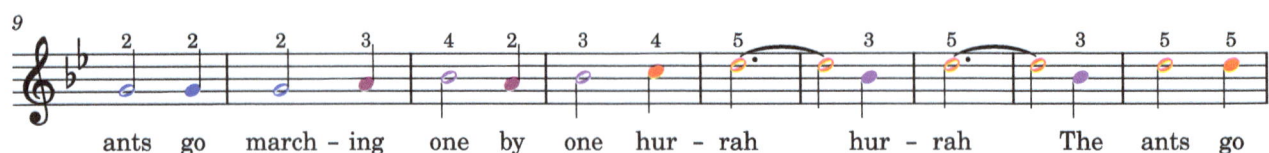
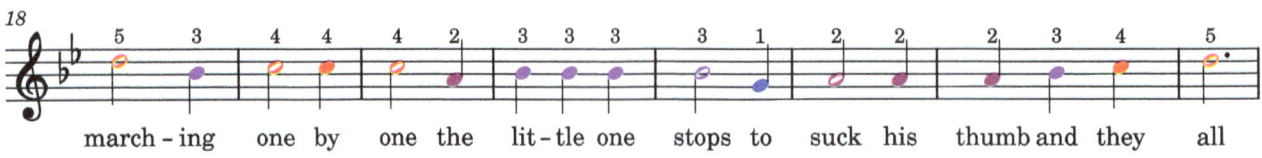
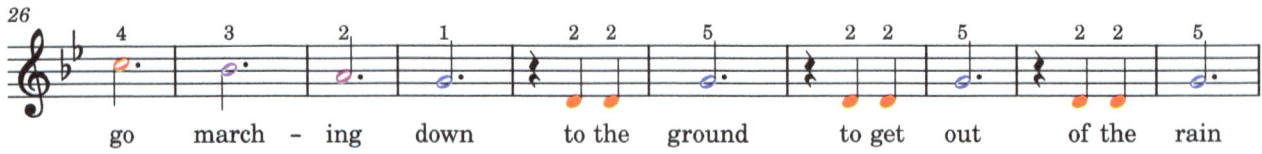
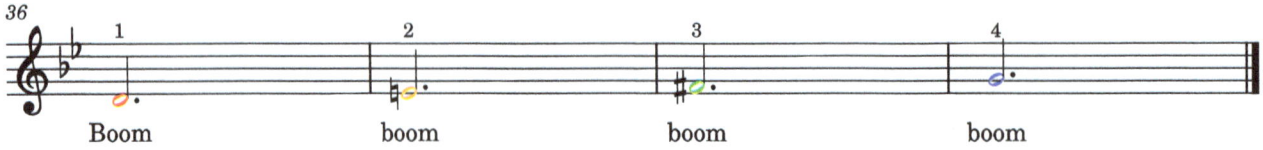

IT'S RAINING, IT'S POURING

Suddenly, a large river split their path and the sky darkened. It began to rain heavily. They sought shelter under a large tree nearby and saw a warm, glowing cottage in the distance. They heard the comforting song coming from it with the words "It's Raining, It's Pouring." Feeling inspired, they played the melody on their piano, and then sang the tune as they walked towards the cottage.

IT'S RAINING, IT'S POURING

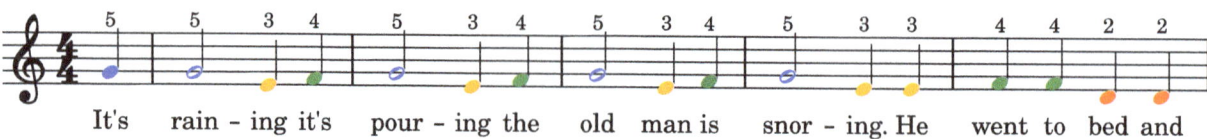

ITSY BITSY SPIDER

Although they knocked on the cottage door, no one answered! That's when they noticed an itsy bitsy spider climbed up a water spout, singing a familiar tune. The spider taught the children the song "Itsy Bitsy Spider" and showed them the secret knock to the forest witch's house. The children thanked the kind spider and knocked with the secret knock.

ITSY BITSY SPIDER

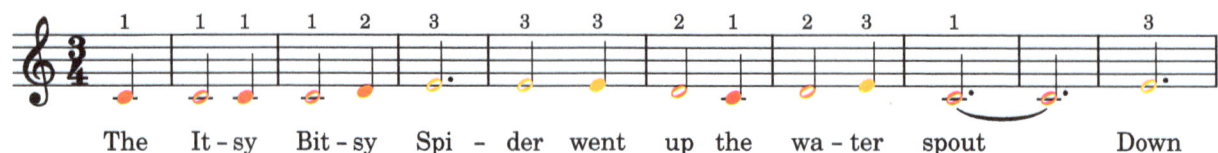
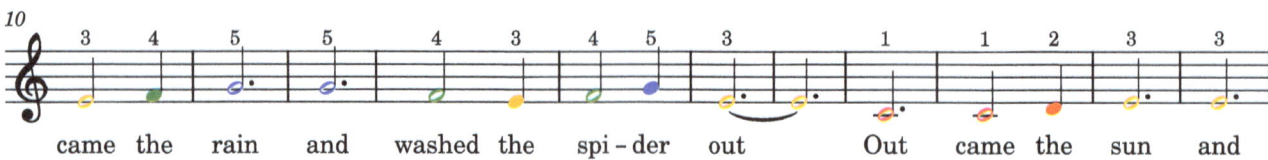
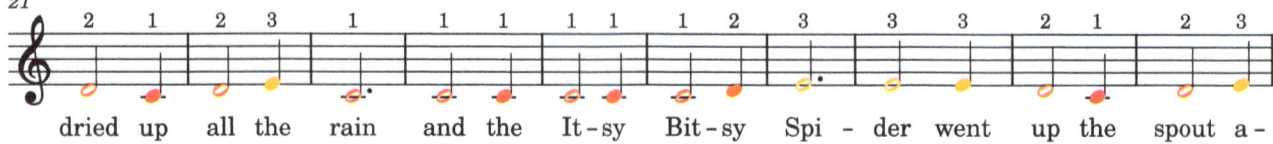
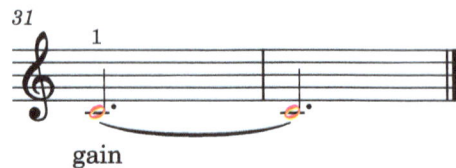

ROW ROW ROW YOUR BOAT

The forest witch opened the door with a smile, welcomed them, and showed them how to build a magical boat. As they crafted their boat, she taught them "Row Row Row Your Boat." The children played the song on their piano as they set off on the river, the music guiding them gently downstream.

ROW ROW ROW YOUR BOAT

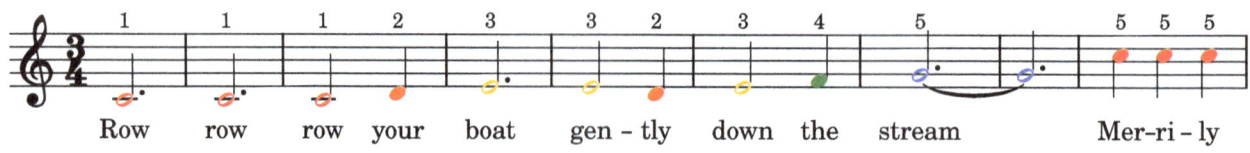

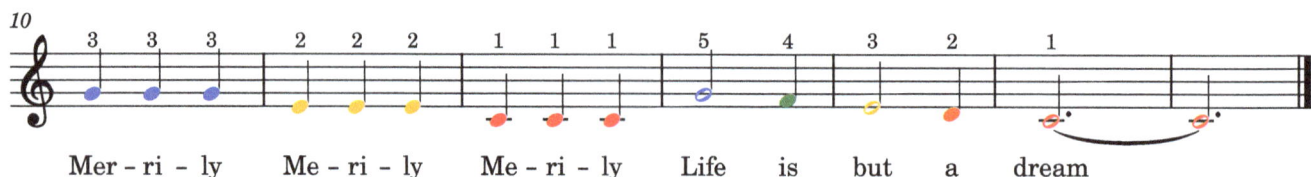

YOU ARE MY SUNSHINE

The rain cleared as they reached the end of the river, and the children found themselves in a large pasture filled with bright, singing tulips. The tulips sang "You Are My Sunshine," and the children played along on their piano, the cheerful tune bringing sunshine into their hearts.

YOU ARE MY SUNSHINE

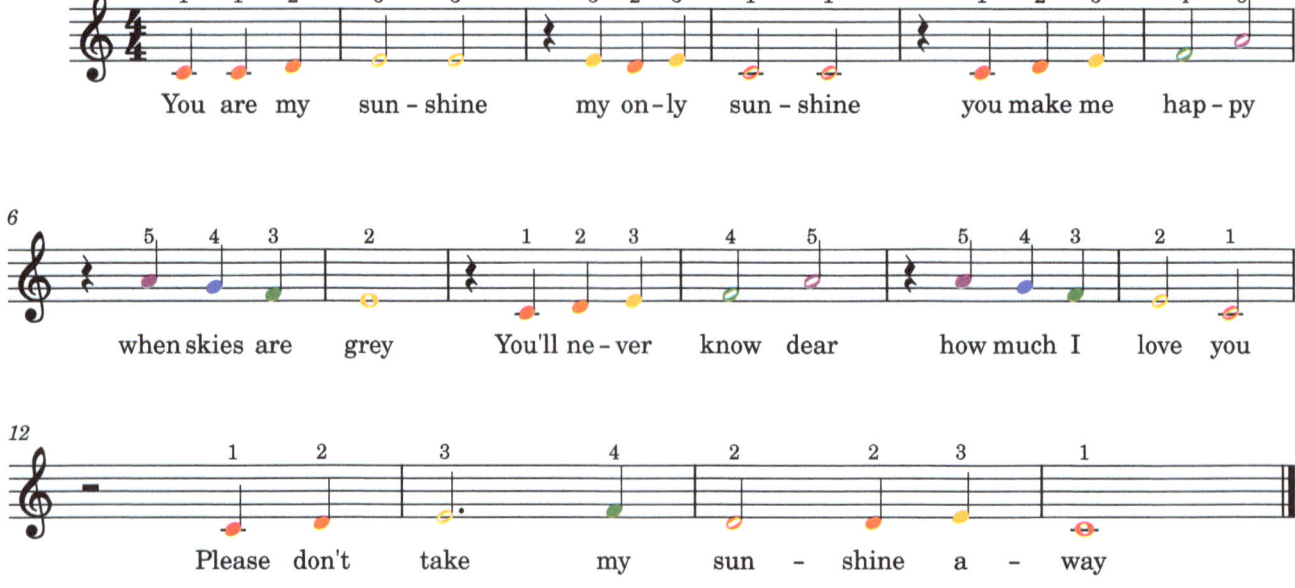

TAKE ME OUT TO THE BALLGAME

After learning all the magical songs, the tulips encouraged the children to share their music with the world. The children returned home and, inspired by their adventure, went to a baseball game. There, they played "Take Me Out to the Ballgame" for everyone to hear, spreading the joy and magic of their musical journey far and wide.

TAKE ME OUT TO THE BALLGAME

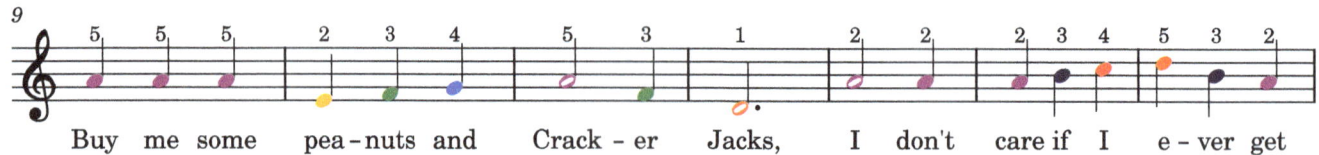
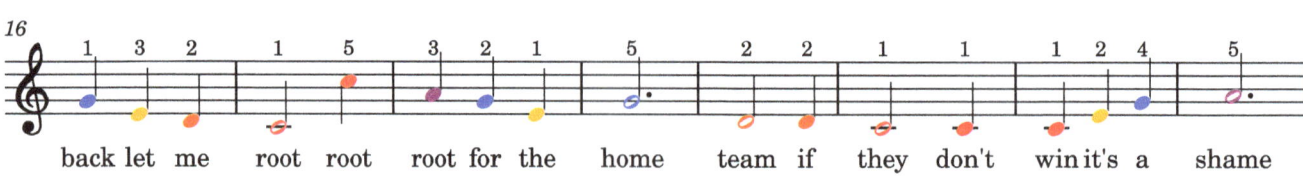
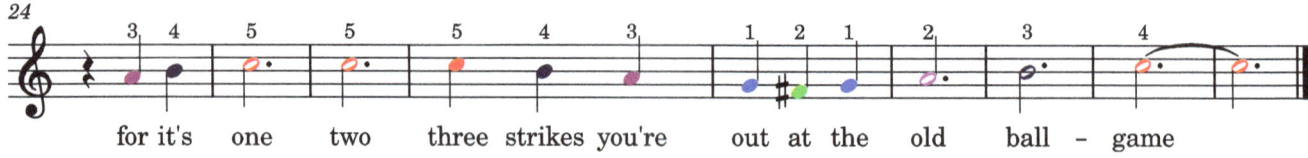

www.ingramcontent.com/pod-product-compliance
Lightning Source LLC
Chambersburg PA
CBHW061355010526
44107CB00012B/940